BOOK 2
Short
E

W9-AUE-906

Disney · PIXAR

THE GOOD DINOSAUR
They Get Away

ISBN: 978-1-338-12827-7

10 9 8 7 6 5 4 3 2 1   16 17 18 19 20

Printed in Malaysia 106

First Printing, September 2016

Scholastic Inc.

Look at Arlo's **egg**.
It is the biggest in the **nest**.

Look at Arlo.
He is smaller than the **rest**.

Buck **gets** to make his mark.
Libby **gets** to make hers too.

Arlo does not **get** to **yet**.
His dad gives him a **test**.

There is a **pest**.
The **pest** is stealing the corn.

Arlo's dad **tells** him to **get** the **pest**.

Arlo **gets** the **pest**!

He **gets** the **pest** in a **net**.

Arlo feels bad for the **pest.**

He **lets** the **pest get** away.

The **pest** and Arlo become friends.

The **pest helps** Arlo **get** berries.

The **pest helps** Arlo.

He **helps** Arlo **get** away!

Arlo names the **pest**.
He calls him Spot.
Arlo and Spot are **best** friends!